the
TOP
of
THE HILL

by Morris Taylor

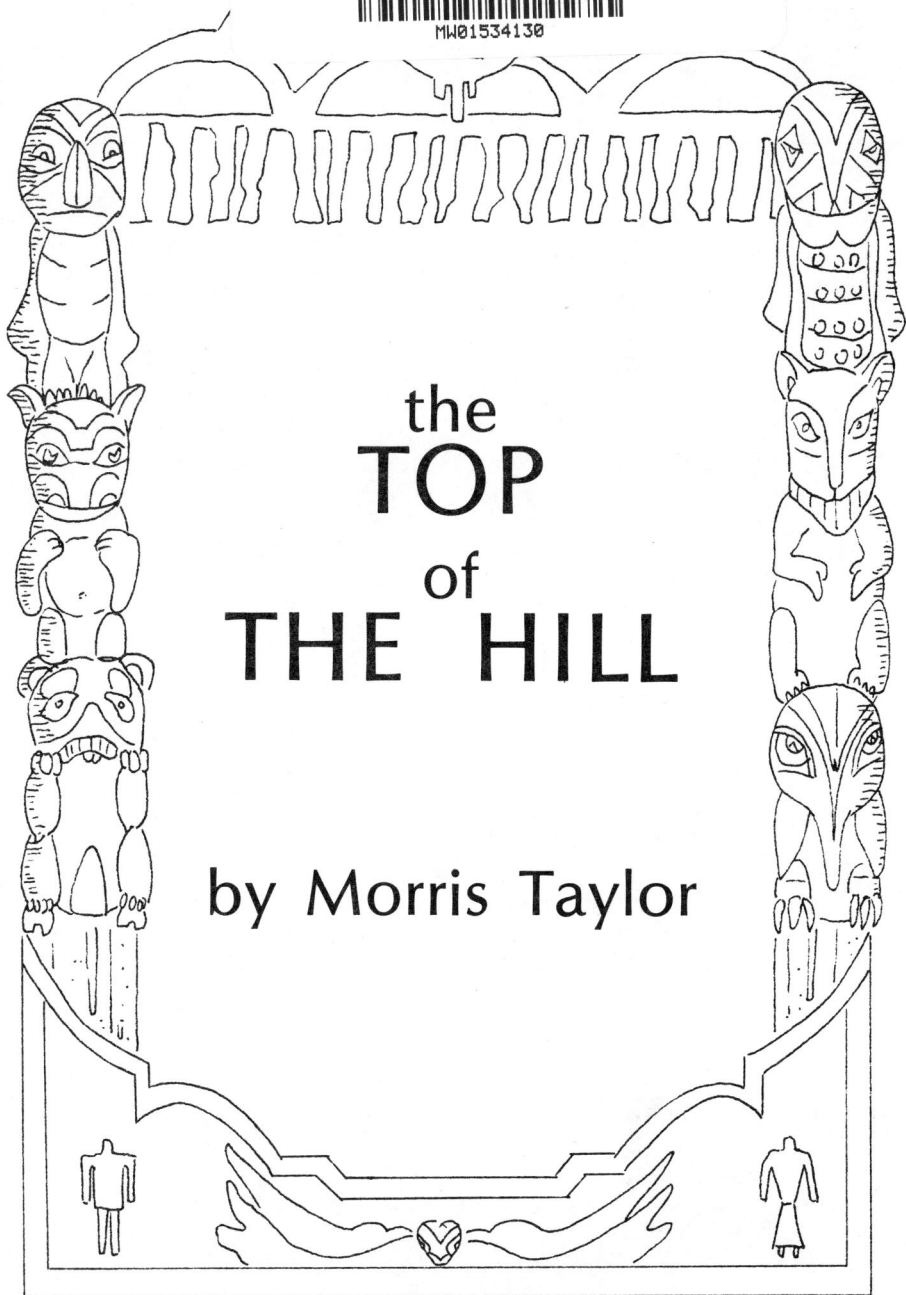

Library of Congress Cataloging in Publication Data

Taylor, Morris
    The Top of the Hill.

ISBN: 0-87961-183-9

Illustrations by Morris Taylor.

Naturegraph Publishers, Inc.
3543 Indian Creek Road
Happy Camp, CA 96039
U.S.A.

Books for a better world

PROLOGUE

Situated a short distance from the reservation was a sparkling river where Red Feather often stopped on the way to and from his third grade class at the government school. The river was exactly halfway between the school and his home on the Arapaho reservation and every morning and afternoon he stopped to skip stones across the surface of the water, a skill at which he was quite good. But on this afternoon as he stood on the riverbank and gazed into the endless sky, Red Feather did not look for the small flat stones that were perfect for skipping. Although today was the last day of the school year and he looked forward to the long summer vacation, his mind was agitated and he did not feel peaceful inside. Something was wrong—frighteningly wrong—and Red Feather somehow knew that this summer would be unlike any other summer that had come before.

Of course, some things would be the same. He would play stickball and eat ice cream and he would almost certainly go to the movie theatre more than once this summer. But something different was going to happen too—something not easily understood. He was not sure why he felt this way, but he thought it had something to do with Great Grandfather.

Red Feather's great grandfather was a medicine man. His name was Dark Sky and his years were so many that none of the people living on the reservation could remember him in any way except as the old man he was now. It was Dark Sky who chose Red Feather's name when he was born eight years ago. In summers past when school was closed, Dark Sky often woke him at dawn and they would watch the sun rise and then take long hikes in the mountains. He taught Red Feather which plants and fruits were safe to eat, and together they fished and built small animal traps which were greatly admired by everyone else on the reservation because few of them remembered how to do such things.

And Dark Sky told many stories—stories about the ancestors and the way they lived long ago.

For years Dark Sky lived in the trailer home with the rest of Red Feather's family, but when he became ill he moved into the large rawhide tent of his youth and refused to come out. This had not worried Red Feather at first; but lying on his cot late one night he overheard some of the adults talking. They said that Dark Sky wanted to be alone for a reason. They spoke of him preparing for a great journey. "Dark Sky may never get well," someone said. "Perhaps he has decided to climb to the top of the hill."

Dark Sky was a medicine man and everyone knew it was very difficult to stop a powerful medicine man from doing what he wished to do once he decided it was necessary. Red Feather didn't know what was meant by "the top of the hill," but he knew that if Great Grandfather had decided to leave him and go away, he had to find a way to stop him. If he could not stop him he would follow Great Grandfather—no matter where he planned to go.

Red Feather's mind would not be still and all of these thoughts were with him as he retrieved his books from the riverbank. Slowly he climbed the grassy incline towards home and the extraordinary summer that would terrify and then transform him.

ONE

First it should be understood that Dark Sky was a medicine man—some said the most powerful medicine man the Arapaho had ever seen. He understood the healing methods of the ancestors—the use of massage, sweat lodges and mud baths, decoctions of barks, pinewood air and smoke—and he used them often to heal others as well as himself.

Secondly, he never drank alcohol, which he said was a great enemy of the spiritual powers, and he smoked the pipe only during special ceremonies.

Hence, Red Feather had never known Dark Sky to be seriously ill. He had never before seen a hospital doctor come to the reservation to examine Dark Sky. Never until this summer.

The changes in Dark Sky were not sudden, nor were they easy to detect. They occurred slowly, gradually. One day his vision was blurred; on the next, his hands did not seem to be as strong as the day before. Little by little his gait slowed and his breathing became ragged. Though he still laughed, he did not laugh as loudly or as often as in summers past.

Red Feather noticed all these things in the month of June. So did David Austin.

David Austin was three years older than Red Feather. He lived in town next door to Red Feather's Aunt Louise, in a house that was shaped like a Navajo hogan. The house was made of orange stone and had a front stoop where David often sat and noticed many important things in the world.

It was the first weeks of summer. Elbows and knees had been skinned and were already well on the way to healing, and faces were browning rapidly in the warm June sun. Early one afternoon, Red Feather and David took a hike to the top of a tall mesa. It was while they stopped to eat a lunch of tuna sandwiches and orange soda that David Austin said, "You know, your great grandpa didn't know me yesterday."

"What do you mean?" asked Red Feather defensively. "He knows you."

David picked up a stone and tossed it high into the air. It returned to the earth with a loud "thwack!" "I know he knows me, but when I came over to your house yesterday he didn't know it was me. He asked me if I was Len Howard!"

"I don't believe you!"

David laughed. "I had to tell him it was me!"

"Stop laughing. He was just fooling you!"

David laughed harder. "He wasn't foolin'! He couldn't *see* me!"

"He must have had something in his eye . . !"

Just as suddenly as the subject had been raised

it was dropped and David Austin chattered about the various colors of snakes in summer. But Red Feather did not speak again and he hiked down from the top of the mesa in silence.

* * *

When Dark Sky isolated himself in the rawhide tent, several of the adults on the reservation began to take turns looking in on him. They made sure that he ate regularly and rested as the doctor had instructed. Red Feather's sister Viola was one of the adults who looked in on Dark Sky each day. She lived in the trailer home with Red Feather and their father. Tall and slender with long dark hair, she was much older than Red Feather yet somehow mysteriously wise in the care of small boys feverish in the summer's heat.

One day very late in June, she stood outside carefully hanging clothes to dry in the afternoon breeze. As she reached for a large sheet, Red Feather handed her a clothespin. She smiled. "How are you today, little brother?"

"I'm fine," sighed Red Feather even though his feeling of discomfort was stronger than ever and he still did not know what it meant.

"You have been very quiet these last several days. Is something wrong?"

Red Feather handed her another clothespin. "Great Grandfather is very old isn't he?"

Viola nodded. "Yes. I have heard some say that Dark Sky was a young child when the holy man Wovoka brought the Ghost Dance to the Piautes. Others say he was a tall youth when General Custer was defeated at the battle of Little Big Horn by the Sioux, Cheyenne, and Arapaho tribes. If that is true, Great Grandfather is more than 100 years old. That is why he is so wise—he has lived a long time and he understands the ways of the ancestors." Viola smiled at her brother. "You have grown into a strong eight-year-old, listening to Dark Sky's wonderful stories."

Red Feather thought for a moment and decided not to speak of his uneasiness for he did not wish to worry Viola. Instead he asked, "May I go to see Great Grandfather?"

Viola looked at him. "Yes. But you must remember that he is not well. The doctor says the infection in his lungs is very serious and he needs a lot of rest. If he is awake you may visit for a very short time, but that is all."

"I won't stay long," said Red Feather looking across the yard towards the tent.

"Good." Viola smiled again. "And do not be so glum. All will be well soon."

Red Feather walked quietly to the tent, considerate not to make any noise as his sneakers pawed the sparse grass. When he reached the tent he pulled back the flap and slipped inside, carefully reclosing the opening and letting in as little light as possible.

In the cool darkness of the tent Red Feather stood motionless and allowed his eyes to adjust to the dim light. Slowly he began to recognize all of Dark Sky's personal possessions which had been carefully placed around the interior of the tent.

A ceremonial shirt and cuffs, decorated with bead and quill work, lay atop a wooden chest. Red Feather wondered for what upcoming occasion Dark Sky intended to wear them. Great Grandfather would not unpack these things without a very special reason, Red Feather thought to himself.

To the left side of the tent, a low metal cot was positioned and upon it, beneath blankets of many bright colors, Dark Sky lay sleeping. The deep wrinkles of age, glistening with perspiration, showed clearly on his face.

Red Feather looked at Dark Sky with quiet uneasiness. He watched the blankets above his chest as they slowly expanded with air, then quickly fell as Dark Sky exhaled in short, uneven breaths. Looking at Dark Sky's deep, copper toned skin, Red Feather was reminded of the story he had been told by his family of how Dark Sky used to cleanse his skin with berry juice to disguise his man-smell, and then sit in a forest clearing. As he made soft whistling sounds in his throat, all of the birds and animals nearby would come to him and gather at his feet. Dark Sky said this was a family reunion of great spiritual power; all of the brothers of the earth gathered together in harmony and peace while still in this world.

Red Feather wanted to jostle Dark Sky and see his eyes open and the familar smile cross his face. He wanted Great Grandfather to play a game of checkers, hike in the mountains or teach him a new chant or prayer. He wanted to laugh and sing and he wanted Dark Sky to laugh and sing with him like he used to do before this summer.

Red Feather sighed and turned to leave.

"Is that you, Red Feather?" A voice whispered in the cool darkness.

Red Feather gasped as he looked towards the cot.

"How is my great grandson?" said Dark Sky.

Red Feather knelt at the side of the cot. "Your great grandson is well, Great Grandfather. But please don't speak. Viola and the others would be angry if they knew I had awakened you."

Dark Sky was breathing loudly and the sound of air rushing in and out of his lungs was as ragged as the dry wind. "You are right. Viola and the others would be angry," He said. "But I wish to speak with my great grandson. Shall they command me otherwise?"

"No," said Red Feather and he smiled because he knew it was useless to disagree with a powerful medicine man.

"Then we shall speak," said Dark Sky. "Help me to sit up."

Red Feather wrapped his arms around the thick blankets and helped Dark Sky to sit upright. He padded more blankets behind his back and helped him cross his weak legs so that he could sit comfortably.

"That is good, Red Feather. Now please open the tent flap that I might see. Yes . . . that is good. Let me rest in this way for a moment, then we will talk."

Red Feather returned to the side of the cot and sat silently looking down at the brown dirt floor of the tent.

As the tepid breeze caught the long, white hair that fell past his brow and shallow cheeks, Dark Sky began to gently rock from side to side. Softly he spoke. "Where have you been? I have not seen you for many days. Is something wrong?"

Red Feather shifted nervously. "No, Great Grandfather."

Dark Sky looked at him, his eyes narrowing into piercing slits. "What is wrong, Red Feather? Do you not want to see me anymore?"

"No, Great Grandfather. I . . . I just thought . . ." Red Feather looked away to avoid the eyes which held him stationary. "I thought I should not bother you because you have been ill."

Dark Sky nodded approvingly. "I see. But you must come to visit me more often. You are the only medicine I want now." Dark Sky rubbed his wrinkled face with the long, narrow fingers of his hand. "When you entered I was not asleep. I was thinking about my own father. Long ago, when I was your age, he said to me, 'You must make your life beautiful like the rainbow.' I have never forgotten this. I have tried to do that with my life . . ." For a moment Dark Sky looked very sad; then his eyes flashed and he smiled. "Look here. I have something for my great grandson."

Dark Sky took Red Feather's hand and pressed something flat and rough into his palm.

Red Feather looked at the object. "The special arrowhead from your father!"

"Yes," said Dark Sky. "It is yours now."

Red Feather gingerly fingered the sharp point.

"But why are you giving this to me?"

"This arrowhead belonged to my ancestors. It has always helped me to feel close to them. I no longer have need of it. It is yours now."

Red Feather regarded the arrowhead proudly. "I will take good care of it. I will feel closer to the ancestors now, too."

Dark Sky laughed. "Good, good. Now perhaps you should go. Viola will be concerned if you stay longer."

Red Feather put the precious arrowhead into his jeans pocket. "I will come back soon," he said. "And thank you for the arrowhead."

Red Feather slipped out of the tent and closed the flap entrance. Great Grandfather is so wise and kind, he thought. Surely he would not go away and leave the ones who love him. As Red Feather walked away from the tent he suddenly heard the rhythmic sound of Dark Sky chanting:

"I did not fear the wind in my life,
I am brother to the earth.
I did not fear the rain in my life,
I am brother to the earth.
The broken pottery returns to dust,
But my soul continues on the Spirit Path;
I am brother to the earth
And my heart is at peace."

Red Feather paused to listen. Although he had heard Dark Sky chant many times before, he did not recognize these new words. He did not know that Dark Sky had only recently written them. He did not know that this chant had a special purpose.

TWO

At least once each summer, sometimes twice, Red Feather spent a weekend in town with Aunt Louise.

Red Feather was still a baby and his sister not yet a teenager when their mother died suddenly, so Louise had cared for them while their father worked. Aunt Louise lived in town, only two miles from the reservation, but to stay at her house was a treat for she enjoyed baking pies and cakes and she always kept an ample supply of homemade Navajo fry-bread in her pantry. She was plump and jolly and very proud of her knowledge of the ancestors. Her house was next door to David Austin's, which made everything quite convenient.

Thus, Red Feather was surprised when in the month of July Louise became an enemy.

It was not intentional and she would have been surprised by the thought; but nonetheless she became an enemy, cold and dangerous. For only an enemy would tell you something that made you cry. Only an enemy would ruin summer.

It was the second weekend in July. Red Feather

arrived with his overnight bag on Friday morning. He went to the movie that afternoon and played stickball with his friends behind Louise's house on Friday night. Slipping into the bathroom after the game, Red Feather bathed quickly and put on his pajamas. When he returned to the living room, he found Louise putting linen on the sofa bed for him. She handed him a pillow case and he slid it over his pillow.

"How was the big game?" she asked.

"It was okay. I scored a run. Tomorrow everybody's going to walk to my house to see Great Grandfather. We're going to ask him to chant for us and tell us stories."

Louise looked at Red Feather. "Well that sounds interesting." For a moment she was very quiet. "Climb into bed," she said finally. "I must tell you about Dark Sky."

Something in her voice made Red Feather feel strangely uncomfortable and afraid. He slowly crawled under the covers, hoping that she would forget her plan and simply say good night.

She did not.

"You know that your Great Grandfather has not been well," she said.

"I know that he has an infection in his lungs," reasoned Red Feather. "He has been resting so that he will get well."

Louise nodded in agreement. "That is true. But there is something more. Dark Sky is preparing for a trip. He is *climbing the hill* now. But do not worry. This is something he wishes to do. When this is finished all will be well."

Red Feather quickly forgot his discomfort and looked at Louise eagerly. "When he returns will he be well again? Will he laugh and tell the stories as he has always done?"

Louise nodded in another way. "No, Red Feather. You do not understand. Dark Sky is very old. He has been in this world too long." Louise tilted her head to one side. "You see . . . Dark Sky must *die* now."

For an instant Red Feather stopped breathing, his small lungs less than half full. His body stiffened and his mind raced breathlessly to understand a word that had no place in the perfect month of July, a word that did not belong in a child's summer that was all too brief!

Animals and plants die, he thought. People unknown, strangers like mother—they died a long time ago, long before you knew them. But people that you *know* don't die. People that *you* know . . . don't . . . *die!*

Words spilled rapidly from his mouth. "No, Aunt Louise. Viola says all will be well soon. "You . . . you said he was going on a trip to climb a hill. Everything will be all right then."

"Shhh. You do not understand," Louise repeated "You fear because you do not understand. First you must still your mind. Then I will explain."

Red Feather sat motionless in the bed, desperately trying to quiet the thunder of his heart.

After several moments Louise spoke. "Many times," she said, "on the television and in your books, you have heard of the 'dark spirits' and the 'happy hunting grounds'—is this not so? These are worn out ideas of this world. You should know that the old people did not think like this.

"The ancestors used to teach that when people die they must go over a hill. This world we live in and the world to come are divided by a line. This line is the top of the hill. When a person is very sick, he may begin to climb to the top of the hill. The climb is very hard and difficult. It is especially hard when those the sick person loves in this world call out to him and try to hold him back."

Red Feather looked at Louise but she was staring in another direction.

"If the person is very sick," she continued, "he will keep climbing. He will not look back but will fight with great strength to reach the top of the hill."

Red Feather swallowed with difficulty, his eyes fixed upon the bed sheets. "What happens if he gets to the top of the hill?"

"If he reaches the top," Louise said, "he can see the other side. The slope leading down is easy and it is full of thick green grass and it is very beautiful. At the bottom is a river and across the river is a large camp."

Red Feather shook his head for he still did not understand. "What does this camp mean? What does it have to do with the sick person?"

"The sick person knows many of these people and he loves them," answered Louise. "As soon as the people see him they call out to him, stretch forth their hands and beg him to leave this world and join them in their joy."

"But the sick man is not one of them. Why do they want him?"

"Because it is his time to join them and they knew of his coming," replied Louise. "They have prepared a place for him and there is work waiting for him and many new things for him to learn. He is eager to make this place his new home. But if the people in this world are unwise and afraid because they do not understand the land beyond, their fears mixed with their love for the person is enough to hold him and he will not go. Even though he may be ready, if the living beg him enough they can hold him." Louise turned her head slowly and looked at Red Feather. "Do you understand now?"

Red Feather felt a thickness rising in his throat. He did not want to look into Louise's eyes. "You . . . you are making me cry," he stuttered shamefully because he had never seen his father or the other men in the tribe cry. "I don't want Great Grandfather to die!"

Louise did not change her words. "This is the way of the Great Spirit. Dark Sky must go—this is the reason for his illness." The enemy, cold and dangerous, took his hands in hers. "I am sorry. Great Grandfather will not get well." She kissed him and rubbed his brow. "You are a big boy now; you must understand these things."

Red Feather wiped the tears from his cheeks and lay back pulling the bed sheets up to his chin. Quietly Louise turned off the light—the enemy left the room.

Red Feather closed his tear-rimmed eyes. The room was silent except for the quiet ticking of the wall clock. Although he was tired, a long time passed before Red Feather fell into a deep sleep...

When Red Feather opened his eyes he was surprised to be standing in a large, green field. Overhead, the sun shone brightly in a blue cloudless sky. Red Feather did not understand how night changed to day so quickly or how he got from his bed to this unfamilar place.

As he turned about, looking for some landmark that would tell him where he was, Red Feather suddenly saw a man, all alone in the distance, walking towards a large hill. The man stopped for a moment and gazed up the hill. At that instant Red Feather realized that the man was Dark Sky!

The sight of Dark Sky so far away from the reservation made Red Feather very happy. "Surely Great Grandfather is better now," he thought and he shouted to him. But Dark Sky continued to walk towards the hill, never turning to look in Red Feather's direction.

When Dark Sky reached the foot of the hill he slowly began to climb towards the top. Red Feather could tell that the climb was steep and very difficult, but Dark Sky did not stop and soon he reached the crest of the hill. Without pausing, Dark Sky walked over the hill and disappeared from sight.

Red Feather did not know where Dark Sky was going but he knew he was somewhere behind the hill. "I will follow Great Grandfather," he thought,

but when he tried to lift his feet he found that they were firmly rooted to the earth, incapable of taking even a single step. In desperation he called out Dark Sky's name once more, but now the wind was blowing loudly and his voice could not be heard. So Red Feather stood helplessly and waited for Dark Sky to return from the far side of the hill.

The morning turned to early evening but Dark Sky did not return. The crest of the hill was void except for the yellow and green grass waving to and fro in the strong winds. Red Feather tried but could see no large camp filled with people. He could see only the hilltop over which Dark Sky had disappeared and his only knowledge of this mysterious hill was that he could not move to follow.

Dark Sky was gone forever. *Forever!*

Red Feather awoke and blinked his eyes. He sat up in the sofa bed. "Oh, I've been dreaming," he thought silently and he yawned. Already the details of the dream were fading from his mind.

But the thought of death did not fade and as he lay back in the bed his fear grew more intense. "Animals die. Strangers die before you know them. But people you know don't die. People you *know* don't die!

"Do they?"

THREE

David Austin was eleven years old and a very important person in Red Feather's life.

Tall and red-headed with soft brown eyes and a freckled nose, David Austin was always full of fun and laughter. He loved baseball and comic books and ice cream sandwiches. And he was Red Feather's best friend.

They never played on separate stickball teams, always defended one another on the school yard, rarely argued and never fought. Candy was shared and girls mutually avoided. It was a perfect friendship.

In the heat of summer, after suppers were eaten, Red Feather and David would race to the cool stoop of the town drug store. There they would sit under the dark canvas awning, watching the people go in and out, and they would fretfully count the days until it was time to put away soiled sneakers, strap on new leather shoes, and return to school. Now, David and Red Feather lay still in the sunburnt grass of David's front yard watching the first wave of early evening fireflies cavort in their helicopter hoverings. Up, down down down; then, as if attached to taut, elastic strings—twipp!—the fireflies shot up into the night darkness.

Red Feather took a deep breath. "David? Hey David, I want to ask you something important."

David stared blankly into the sky. "Just listen to that. Wow!" He rose up on one elbow. "Crickets, crickets and more crickets! They chirp, they crackle, they pop. Hundreds of 'em, thousands—maybe a zillion! Altogether, in unison, rubbing their wings like violins and big bass fiddles. Crickets and cicadas, a summer symphony, a whole orchestra in our own front yard. Wow!"

Red Feather listened for a moment. "Violins and bass fiddles?"

"Yeah!"

There was a moment of silence. "You know what?"

"What?"

"You need to have your ears checked."

Red Feather giggled and tried to roll away before David's wiry grasp could entangle him. They laughed together and for a while rolled wildly over the dry grass and three leaf clovers. Red Feather laughed loudly. It was easy to forget the panic he had felt the night before and which had haunted him throughout the day; easy to forget that all was not as it should have been in this uncertain summer.

Red Feather landed on top, his breathing heavy and deep. "David. Really . . . I need to ask you something."

David stopped struggling and pulled away from him. For a moment Red Feather thought he was listening but suddenly, in a breath, David lashed out an arm towards the dark sky. Red Feather reached to grab him again.

"Hold it a minute, Red Feather, hold it! I got one!"

Red Feather released his grip and looked at David's balled fist. "What have you got?"

"A firefly!" David cupped his hands together and held them like a small treasure chest, only a tiny crack between his thumbs. "Looky here. See that?"

Red Feather looked. Inside the "chest," a tiny light flickered on then off. "Fireflies must be magic. How else could they have those little lights that flash on and off? When you walk around at night, one minute there's nothing there and the next minute there they are, all around you, lights out of nowhere. I think it must be magic!"

"Sure! Hey yeah!" David closed the crack and held it tight. "Magic! Fireflies in mayonaise jars. They'd make great flashlights late at night. Just think—magic pets that shine and glow on and off all night long!"

Red Feather scratched his ear. "It's not important right now, David. Listen, I want to ask you about . . ."

"We'll find out!" David leapt to his feet and ran towards the house. "I'll get a jar. You catch some more of 'em. I'll be right back!" Red Feather watched him as David entered the front door then bumped it shut with his hip, all the while clutching the magic light so that it would not slip away.

Several minutes later, the crickets and cicadas hidden in the shrubbery around the house momentarily grew silent as David bounded back down the front steps. In one hand he gripped a wide mouth glass jar with a metal top. Inside the jar was the magic light he had captured. "Hey, Red Feather! Red Feather, where are you?"

Red Feather appeared from beneath the dark mulberry tree at the edge of the lawn. He walked very slowly, his two fists clenched, loosely imprisoning the delicate creatures hidden deep within the folds of dark skin. "I caught five of them but you should count them." He drew close and examined the jar with his eyes. "Wait . . . there are no holes in the top."

"Huh?" David looked at him. "Whatcha' need holes for? You want 'em to escape?"

"They have to breathe, David."

David stared at Red Feather's clenched fists. "Yeah . . . I guess they do. But there's enough air in there for now. We'll punch holes in there later. First let's see if they'll work." He reached out and took hold of one of Red Feather's wrists. "All right. Here's one . . . two in the jar. There's three . . ."

Red Feather brushed his open hand against his pants leg and extended the other.

"Four . . . five . . . hey you got six. Good job!"

"I'm not too sure about this, David." Red Feather said softly.

David twisted the metal top tightly into place.

"Not sure about what?"

"Putting the fireflies into jars. It doesn't seem right."

David moved quickly towards the front porch steps, Red Feather trailing slowly behind him. He set the jar of fireflies on the stoop and sat staring into the glass. "What don't seem right about it?"

"Well . . ."

"What's wrong with it huh? I'm listenin'. Ain't nothin' wrong. We won't hurt 'em; we won't touch 'em. Just gonna' use 'em. Maybe I'll tie a string around one of them and let him fly ahead of me at night! Wow, look at that big one there!"

"Where? Let me see." They both leaned close to the jar.

Red Feather stared at the lights hovering silently near the top of the jar. He bit his lip as he watched one float to the bottom, circle the perimeter as if searching for a way out, then fly back to the top. He swallowed hard. "I'm going to get a glass of water from your mother," he said rising.

"Huh?"

"A glass of water . . ." He opened the screen door.

"Oh . . . me too. Wait up."

They slammed the front door, leaving the jar behind on the stoop.

The symphony of crickets and cicadas, all but invisible in the shrubs, reached it's evening crescendo and began to dissipate. The July breeze grew cooler.

Soon David bounced onto the stoop and fell to

one knee in front of the jar. Red Feather stood in the shadows of the doorway but did not come out. He could not see the jar from where he was but he noticed that David was strangely quiet.

"Hey! Hey, Red Feather, somethin's wrong. Come here and look."

Red Feather shut the door and descended the steps. He turned to face the jar.

The inside of the jar was dark and seemingly empty. At the bottom, seven tight black balls lay apart, unmoving, around the circle's edge.

"Are they dead?"

David shook the jar timidly. He tilted it to one side. All of the balls rolled together and lay still in a heap. "I don't get it. What happened?"

"They must be dead." Red Feather stared at the lifeless balls. His stomach tightened. "They must have *suffocated.* I told you to put holes in the top. How are they going to breathe without holes? I *told* you . . ."

David unscrewed the top and waited for something to happen. He shook the jar again, exhaling heavily. "No use keepin' 'em." He set the jar down in the grass. "I guess we'll have to use regular lights like everybody else."

Red Feather leaned back in the grass, trying hard not to show his despair over the fate of the helpless fireflies. "Maybe it was just a bad idea."

David looked at the jar wistfully and sat down beside him. "Yeah, a bad idea." They both lay still on the lawn, the symphony gradually diminishing in their ears.

Across the street a child ran laughing down the sidewalk. Auto headlights passed the house and disappeared around a corner. The evening grew late.

David took a quiet breath of the darkness. "Red Feather?"

Across the warm night air Red Feather answered. "Yes?"

"Your great grandpa still sick?"

Red Feather paused long enough to sit up on his elbows. "Yes. But he has been resting a lot. I think he will be well soon."

"My mom says he's gonna' die," David said matter-of-factly.

Red Feather did not speak.

"Too bad we can't live forever," David continued. "It's kind of weird—I guess it's just your great grandpa's time to go."

Red Feather turned to David in the darkness, anger invading his voice. "He is not going to die."

David laughed in a way that seemed cruel. "You don't have to get mad or nothin'. It happens to everybody. Dogs, horses, people. He's old that's all. And he's gonna' die."

"I said he is not going to die!" Red Feather shouted. *"He is not going to die!"*

"You boys?" Behind them the stoop light flashed on. "What's all that shouting?" David's mother opened the screen door and peered out.

"Ain't nothin', Ma."

"Well, time for you to come in, David. Tell Red Feather good night."

David stood up, brushing the grass from his trousers. "I gotta' go. See you later." David entered the house. After a moment the front door slammed shut. The stoop light faded.

Red Feather sat alone in the grass, staring out into the dark streets. "Everybody has to die. Dogs, horses, people . . ." He repeated the words in his mind. "Everybody has to die. But if everybody has to die, that means someday even . . . *Great Grandfather!* If *everybody* has to die, that means even . . . even . . . !"

Red Feather looked at his hands. They were warm hands, supple hands. Hands that had thrown baseballs and held kittens. Hands that had lit fire crackers on the fourth of July and hands that had wiped sweat from his brow and felt safe and secure when he dug them deep into the covers at night to sleep. He tried to imagine his hands stiff and cold, never, ever, to move again.

A cold feeling traveled down his spine.

Red Feather slowly rose to his feet. Crossing the lawn he climbed the steps of Louise's house. Pausing at the door, he turned to look back into the night.

The summer symphony had ended; the small children were asleep. The only sound that met his ears was the high-pitched drone of the neon street lamps.

Red Feather entered the house and shut the door.

* * *

Across the street on David's lawn, a tight black ball stirred to life at the bottom of the topless mayonaise jar. A tiny light, golden and warm, flickered and began to glow in the darkness. Another light appeared, then another, and fragile wings started to flutter like the batting of eyelashes several times over.

In slow motion seven fireflies rose delicately into the air. For several moments they hovered over the open jar, then rapidly disappeared into the warm July night.

FOUR

On Sunday morning, Red Feather awoke early to eat breakfast with Louise. When they were done, he kissed her good-bye, and carrying his overnight bag he slowly walked across the front lawn towards the vast fields which separated the town from his home on the reservation.

As he passed the tall buttes and mesas, rich orange and brown in the bright morning light, Red Feather thought deeply about the things Aunt Louise and David had told him. Now he felt more uncomfortable than ever. Death was still a mystery, strange and fearful, and in his heart he knew that he would never be happy until the mystery was solved. But as he neared the reservation he felt something else in his heart, and suddenly he was filled with hope.

Red Feather knew there was one person— someone he loved and trusted very much—who would surely tell him the truth. This person was old and very wise and Red Feather's heart began to sing for now he knew where he would go to solve the mystery of death.

When Red Feather reached home the reservation was quiet as it often was on Sunday mornings. Many of the people had gone to town and only a few of the older tribes people and some of the children stayed behind.

Red Feather knew Viola was baking bread as she always did on Sundays and he walked directly towards Dark Sky's tent behind the trailer.

He approached the closed tent as quietly as he could in case Great Grandfather might be sleeping. But as Red Feather drew nearer he heard Dark Sky's voice. It sounded very old and weak and Red Feather listened closely. Dark Sky was chanting the strange chant which Red Feather had now heard several times.

". . . *The broken pottery returns to dust,*
But my soul continues on the Spirit Path;
I am brother to the earth
And my heart is at peace."

As Red Feather stood listening, rehearsing his words and the many questions he would ask Dark Sky, he suddenly felt very ashamed.

How could he, a small boy, dare to ask a wise and brave medicine man about such a thing as fear? How could he think that Great Grandfather might understand the empty feeling in the pit of his stomach or the strange discomfort that had grown so strong and that now seemed to always be with him? No, Great Grandfather would not understand the fear of a young boy.

And yet Red Feather desperately wanted to see Dark Sky. He wanted to sit with him and listen to the wise words which always made him feel better. So Red Feather gently called out to him. "Great Grandfather? Great Grandfather?"

The chanting stopped. "Red Feather?" Dark Sky's voice sounded as if he were smiling. "Please come in."

Red Feather opened the tent flap and stepped inside.

Dark Sky was sitting cross-legged on the dirt floor. In one hand he held a rattle and in the other he held a string of colored prayer beads which he used to count the repetitions of his chants. Dark Sky looked small and frail, but his eyes appeared to dance and sparkle like bright jewels. "The morning light is good," he said. "Open the flap as wide as you can and come join me."

Red Feather opened the flap then sat cross-legged upon the floor. He did not speak.

Dark Sky's eyes stopped dancing. He looked at Red Feather in a serious way. "Why are you disheartened these days? You are always full of joy and happiness and now you sit like the Buffalo Dance costume against the wall—spiritless and without power of its own. Is there something you wish to say to me?"

Red Feather tried not to look unhappy. "There is nothing I wish to say, Great Grandfather."

Dark Sky lay the rattle and colored beads to one side. Red Feather did not look up but he knew Dark Sky was studying his face.

Finally Dark Sky spoke in a solemn voice. "For several weeks I have been watching you," he said.

"In the past you have always come to me. You brought your problems, your fears, the mysteries of childhood which you could not understand and I helped you. But in the life of each child there comes a time when he must seek the greater wisdom. I sense that time has come for you."

For several moments Dark Sky stared silently at Red Feather. Then, he raised his weak hand and pointed to something outside the tent. Red Feather looked and he saw that Dark Sky was pointing to a range of mountains a few miles beyond the reservation.

"On the day after tomorrow the sun will be mid-way on its journey to the south. The power of the spirit will be strong and the mountain and all that lives within it will vibrate with its influence. If you cannot share your burden with those who love you, then you must share it with the One Above. You must go to the mountain and seek the guidance that will calm your spirit and strengthen it. The time has come for you to seek your first vision, my great grandson."

Red Feather's eyes grew wide. "But Great Grandfather," he stammered, "I don't know how to seek a vision. The boys who seek their first visions are much older than me. I don't know what to do!"

"I will accompany you to the mountain and show you what you must do."

Red Feather sat stunned for a moment then took a deep breath. "I . . . I want to go, Great Grandfather. I do not feel calm inside and perhaps the One Above will help me. I do want to seek my first vision. But how can you go with me? You are not well and you must rest."

"Rest?" Dark Sky chuckled quietly. "There is no reason for me to rest now." Then he said, "In my life I have taken many young men to seek their visions. Many years ago, when your father was only a boy,

trembling and afraid, I took him to find his first vision on the mountaintop. Now the One Above has given me a great gift. He has given me the opportunity to help someone I love very much—He has given me the opportunity to help you." Dark Sky nodded assuringly. "Do not worry. The One Above will give me the strength I need. But first we must both make preparation. Eat a good breakfast tomorrow but do not eat again until I say you may. Begin now to pray that the One Above may purify you and make known to you His ways."

Red Feather rose to his feet. "I will do this. I will chant the prayers you have taught me."

"Good, good." Dark Sky looked again towards the mountains. "Come here tomorrow, very early, and I will explain all you must do. For we will leave tomorrow night. We will sleep beneath the stars and on the next day you will meet the dawn upon the mountaintop."

Red Feather withdrew from the tent and closed the flap. For a long moment he stood still, trying to understand what had just occurred. His hands were cold and damp as he stared at the intricate tent designs painted upon the rawhide in shades of red and brown. All his life he had heard tales of the vision quest and now he was about to embark on his own. He could not imagine what would happen next. He had no idea what to expect once he faced the heavens and asked the One Above to unfold before him the great mystery of death.

FIVE

The sky was the color of apricot gold as dusk settled over the reservation. Red Feather tied his sleeping bag and blankets into a large roll and hastened to meet Dark Sky in the field beyond the trailer court.

After sitting with him throughout the morning and carefully memorizing his rigid instructions, Red Feather had listened nervously as Dark Sky explained to Viola that they were going to camp overnight on the mountain. Viola had objected at first, reminding Dark Sky of the doctor's warnings; but Dark Sky did not waver and, like everyone else, Viola knew it was very difficult to stop a powerful medicine man from doing what he wished to do once he decided it was necessary. After reluctantly giving her consent, Viola's concern was so great that she failed to notice that Red Feather ate neither lunch nor dinner before their departure.

Dark Sky preceded Red Feather as they crossed the open country leading to the foot of the mountains. His steps were slow but deliberate and sure, for he had tread these paths into the mountains many times before. Over his shoulder hung a large leather bag and under his arm he carried a single thin blanket.

In silence Dark Sky walked, Red Feather following behind him respectfully, until they reached a seldom traveled path which led up the side of the mountain.

They paused and Red Feather glanced quickly about. His eyes were well-trained and he could see and hear the mice and other small animals as they scurried out of their path. Only a few feet away, a band of quail huddled beneath the bushes.

"Behold the land of your ancestors," Dark Sky said with great reverence. "Look upon the work of the Great Spirit and know that it is perfect. Only here, in a place that is quiet and isolated from men, can one seek the vision that brings peace to the soul."

The woods were so quiet and still that Red Feather forgot the hunger which gnawed at his stomach. He closed his eyes and listened. "Why is silence so beautiful, Great Grandfather?"

Dark Sky smiled. "When left undisturbed, nature is in a perfect state of balance. Through silence, we are able to communicate with nature and thus we also find the perfect balance of body, mind and spirit. It is this state of inner peace and balance that we call beautiful."

Dark Sky put his hand on Red Feather's shoulder and gazed up the side of the mountain. "Now we begin to ascend the mountain. From this moment on your mind must remain in a state of complete concentration. You must observe silence and keep your mind on spiritual matters and the purpose of your search. Come quickly."

With that Dark Sky began to chant and he slowly ascended the path which led up the mountainside. Red Feather followed in alert anticipation.

The night grew dark yet Dark Sky did not falter for he knew well the path of the mountain. Halfway to their destination, he paused to look back at Red Feather. "You are wondering why it is necessary to fast," he said.

Dark Sky's eyes seemed to glow in the moonlight. Red Feather remained silent but waited curiously for his explaination.

"The body is a reflection of the spirit," Dark Sky said. "If a man can rule his body, he can rule his own spirit and this is a sign of self control and fixed purpose. Prayer and fasting and lonely vigil will induce the good vision." Turning abruptly, Dark Sky continued up the mountain.

Red Feather was very tired and they had climbed a great distance into the sky when Dark Sky stopped suddenly. He pointed several hundred yards away towards a cliff that jutted out from the mountain in dark silouette. "There is where you alone must climb."

As Red Feather visually measured the distance to the cliff, Dark Sky lay his blanket upon the ground and stretched it out flat. Carefully taking the leather bag from his shoulder, he opened it and began to withdraw several items. From the bag he

pulled a large strip of buffalo skin and spread it upon the ground. Upon the skin he placed two rattles, a string of beads, and several eagle feathers. Lastly, he took from the bag a small buckskin pouch which he handled with great care. Red Feather knew the pouch contained the medicine man's possessions which were most sacred and healing.

"Put your sleeping bag and blankets beneath the stone ledge you will find upon the cliff and then follow the instructions I have given you. Do you remember all that I have said?"

Red Feather nodded.

"Good." Dark Sky reached into his leather bag once more and handed Red Feather a bundle folded in white cloth. "All that you need is here. Remember to pray as I have taught you. If you grow tired you may sleep, but you must stay upon the cliff until you have received your vision. I will wait for you here. Do you understand?"

Again Red Feather nodded.

"Good. Now hurry, my great grandson. Hurry to hear what the One Above wishes to say to you!"

Red Feather took a deep breath, then quickly began to climb towards the obscure and dimly visible cliff high above them.

When Red Feather reached the cliff he looked back down the mountain to where he had left Dark Sky. The light of the moon was bright but he could see neither the mountain path nor the trusted friend who waited far below for his return.

Standing alone on the black cliff, Red Feather listened to the wind as it whistled past him and careened aimlessly through the mountains. He was not afraid for he knew the sounds of nature well; yet on this night every noise seemed louder than he had ever heard it before. Snapping, sliding, twisting, oozing, the somber mountain bristled all around him with hidden life.

Red Feather felt certain that every creature on the mountain was strangely aware of his presence and that he did not belong among them. He wanted to shout out, to call to Dark Sky to be sure that he was near. But Red Feather knew he could not do this. All alone, he knew that his only protection lay in faultlessly carrying out the strict instructions Dark Sky had given him.

Red Feather unrolled his sleeping bag and blankets and laid them beneath the low ledge a few yards from the edge of the cliff. With care he unfolded the bundle wrapped in white cloth. Inside were four strips of fabric: one black, one white, one yellow and one red. Each of these he tied to one of four straight sticks of medium length, and the four sticks with the strips of cloth he positioned in a circle, one to the north, one to the south, one to the east and one to the west.

Red Feather stepped into the center of the circle and shut his eyes. Slowly he turned towards the west. Standing perfectly still, he silently prayed for guidance and strength, for courage and humility. When he was done, he returned to the circle's center and then stepped towards the north and prayed again. Then he approached the east and the south, each time praying and each time returning to the center of the circle. When this was done, he turned his face towards the moonlit sky and he prayed to the heavens. Then he turned his eyes to the earth beneath his feet and again he prayed for assistance.

When Red Feather was finished he left the circle and crawled beneath the ledge of rock. He had not planned to sleep but suddenly he felt exhausted and he could not keep his eyes open. He decided to get into his sleeping bag for a few brief moments and then return to his prayers.

As he zipped the bag around his body he heard a familar sound.

Far, far below the cliff, Dark Sky began to chant. Red Feather could hear the rhythmic roll of the rattles and Dark Sky's voice was not weak but strong and clear in the darkness.

Calm and assured, Red Feather lay upon his back. Looking beyond the ledge, he could see the stars through the trees. He closed his eyes.

Throughout the night Red Feather could hear Dark Sky's steady chanting. When he awoke at dawn, the chanting had not stopped but continued in a pulsing beat. Instantly he remembered where he was and for what purpose he had come. Wiping the sleep from his eyes he crawled out from under the ledge and stood erect in the cool mountain air.

In the pale early sunlight he could see out over the plains and fields far below him. For the first time he realized how high above the earth he was.

Red Feather waited several moments to be sure he was wide awake, then ardently he began to pray once more. To the west, north, east and south he prayed; then to the skies above and to the earth below. When he was done he knelt in the center of the circle and listened as the sounds of the mountain and the distant chanting merged and became indistinguishable.

Red Feather momentarily closed his eyes. When he reopened them, he was no longer upon the mountain. He was astonished to be standing in an unfamiliar field very much like the one he had seen in his dream. But he was not dreaming this time. The scene before him was much clearer than any dream and it had a certain glow that convinced him that what was about to happen was the miracle for which he had prayed to the One Above.

Red Feather stood still and waited. When nothing occurred he moved his head slightly and cast a glance over his shoulder. Directly behind him he saw a large grassy knoll like the one he had seen in his dream, and at the top of the knoll, standing tall and erect in a brightly colored blanket, was Dark Sky! Bewildered, Red Feather strained his ears to listen. From a distance far away he could hear the rhythmic hissing of the rattles and Dark Sky's chanting voice on the mountain. He quickly realized that the figure before him was not the real Dark Sky but a part of his vision.

As Red Feather watched, the vision of Dark Sky lifted its arms. But they were not arms—they were large eagle's wings. Then Dark Sky looked to the sky and his face became an eagle's face and beak and when his blanket fell away he had an eagle's

feathered body.

The eagle rose into the sky and began to circle above the grassy hill. In a high, shrill voice the eagle cried out, "Beyond the farthest horizon Dark Sky must go. He must take flight like the eagle and fly away . . . fly away . . . !" The eagle circled once more then disappeared behind the great hill.

The eagle that was Dark Sky was gone from his sight. But Red Feather knew it was on the far side of the hill. "I must follow," he thought. Cautiously he took a step towards the hill. To his surprise his body leapt several feet forward. His next step easily took him to the foot of the hill. Like a wild antelope, graceful and swift, Red Feather effortlessly ran up the side of the hill. His heart nearly burst with joy for at last he was being allowed to follow Dark Sky, no matter where he was going. Eagerly he reached the hill's crest and looked over to the other side.

The crest of the hill was a sharp precipice and far below was a large Indian camp, one unlike any Red Feather had ever seen before.

There were many people in the camp, not just Indians but also whites and blacks and peoples from lands far away. The people were very happy. Children were playing in a river and some of them were on horseback; some of the people were singing and many were laughing. A bright, white light radiated from the camp and the light made Red Feather feel warm and happy and quite suddenly he realized that he was laughing, too.

As Red Feather stood gazing into the camp, he was startled to hear several people behind him;

they were walking towards the crest of the hill. A few of the people seemed confused, but most of them were smiling. Some were holding hands and others were speaking softly and looking ahead eagerly. They passed Red Feather and slowly descended the slope towards the camp of light.

With great happiness Red Feather began to follow but when a few of the people in the camp looked up they stopped laughing and frowned. "No, no!" they called and then everyone in the camp and the people descending the hill looked up and saw him. "No, no!" they all cried together and they motioned him away.

The people shouted louder and louder. Red Feather stopped, frightened and confused.

Suddenly, amidst the shouting, he heard the shrill voice of the eagle. He looked up and saw the great bird circling overhead.

"Do not be despondent," the bird cried. "First Red Feather must strive. Then his heart will grow strong and pure. Strong and pure. Then his heart will grow strong and pure."

Red Feather felt tears welling in his eyes. He did not understand but he knew that he would not be allowed to join the people in the strange camp. As he turned to walk back over the hill he saw standing behind him his sister, Viola. As she stood in the sun her slender figure was framed by the light and a soft brown lustre reflected from her raven black hair.

"I don't understand," said Red Feather softly. "I don't understand," he said again as he blinked his eyes and opened them wide . . .

The large hill was gone. The vision dissolved like vapor on the summer desert. The morning sun had risen high enough to dissipate the shadows on the mountain top and the chanting had stopped.

Dizzy with hunger and thirst, Red feather collapsed inside the circle of four sticks. As he lay motionless upon the ground, he could hear all around him the singing of birds and life within the mountain began to stir and throb.

SIX

Hands.

Familiar hands. Protective hands.

Warm, not cold. Good, not evil. Strong hands that lift and carry. Unfailing hands that do not tire. Hands that delivered him, safe and secure, to his own home, to his own family, to his own bed.

Red Feather lay still trying to recall how he returned from the jagged cliff of the mountain to the reservation. He only remembered being lifted—perhaps over someone's shoulder—and when he awoke he was safe in his bed at home.

Outside, the street lamps which lined the paths of the reservation began to flicker on. Red Feather could hear the voices of people returning from work, slamming pickup truck doors and turning off motorcycle engines, and he knew it was very late in the day. He climbed from the bed and dressed quickly. Heedless of his hunger, he left the trailer in search of Dark Sky. He was anxious to have him interpret the vision and to explain the meaning of the strange things he had seen.

The entrance to Dark Sky's tent was open. As

Red Feather peered into the dim light Dark Sky called out his name. "Red Feather. Come in! Have you eaten? Come in!"

Dark Sky was sitting upright on his cot, a broad smile upon his face. "You slept all day. How do you feel?"

Red Feather smiled. "I am very hungry but I feel fine. I had my vision," he said pleased.

"I know," said Dark Sky. "I am proud of you, my great grandson."

Red Feather sat at his feet. "I do not remember coming down from the mountain. How did I get to my bed?"

Dark Sky laughed. "Did I not tell you the One Above would give me the strength I needed?" he asked. "Now share with me your vision and we will see what the Great Spirit wishes you to understand."

Red Feather took a deep breath before speaking. "Great Grandfather, you are always so kind to me. You always help me when I am confused. I want to tell you everything. I want to tell you that for many days I have been . . . I have been . . ."

"Afraid?" asked Dark Sky.

"Yes," said Red Feather despairingly, "and I am very ashamed."

Dark Sky frowned. "Why are you ashamed? All brave warriors are afraid sometimes. It is not bad to be afraid as long as you do not let your fear destroy you. You conquered your fear by seeking the vision—that is all that matters now. But tell me, what fear drove you to seek the vision?"

Red Feather coughed so that he did not have to

answer right away. Finally he said, "I have been afraid because . . . you are climbing to the top of the hill."

"Oh?" Dark Sky responded with surprise. He looked at Red Feather strangely. "Tell me what you know about the top of the hill."

Red Feather carefully told him what Aunt Louise had said about the climb to the top of the hill. Then he told him of his vision on the mountaintop. He told Dark Sky that he too had been part of the vision and that he had turned into an eagle that spoke strange words. He described the people on the far side of the hill and how they refused to let him follow the eagle and join them in the unusual camp.

When he was done, Dark Sky looked at him with great pleasure. "I know your love for me is very great, but my future is of no importance. Your vision is very good and brings an important message from the One Above. Though it is unclear to you now, there is no need for me to interpret it. All you must do is continue to follow the ways of the spirit and the meaning of your vision will be clear to you in the years to come. That is all I need to say. Now go and eat something or your body will grow weaker." Without another word, Dark Sky shifted his body and turned away.

Red Feather was heartbroken. His lip began to quiver as he fought to control his emotions. "But I'm still afraid!" he cried.

Dark Sky turned about. "But why?"

"Because . . ." Red Feather felt his heart

pounding. "Because I don't want you to die and . . . *I don't want to die!*" he shouted. *"I don't want to die."*

Dark Sky sat as still as a statue and a long silence fell over the tent. During the silence, Red Feather's heart continued to pound and he struggled to hold back his tears.

"I have told you many stories about our people and about the Great Spirit," Dark Sky said softly. "Have I ever told you this story about the top of the hill?"

"No, Great Grandfather—someone else told me."

"Yes. And do you know why I have never told you this?"

Red Feather did not know. "I will tell you why," said Dark Sky. After a pause he said, "Some people believe this world and the world to come are divided by a river and as we cross the river into the next world we can see waiting for us on the other side those who have gone before. Others say we must walk through a dark tunnel and others say that we must travel over a hill. Perhaps it is all of these things; perhaps it is none of them. In truth, no man is certain what form the journey will take. Only those who have gone before fully understand."

Red Feather looked puzzled. "But if no one knows what death is like, why do they tell these stories?"

"These stories have been passed on from father to son, from one generation to the next, because they teach an important truth. Many men think that they are only muscle and bone, frail bodies that must grow old and someday die. But these stories teach us that we are more than this. We are spirit, eternal souls that cannot die."

Red Feather hesitated for a moment. "What do *you* think death is like, Great Grandfather?"

Dark Sky smiled. "I think the Great Spirit in His wisdom does not want us to know everything about the journey called death or where it will take us until it is time for us to go. Foolish people lead selfish lives, never giving of themselves to help others because they fear that death brings a terrible end. But for those who strive to live their lives in the way of the spirit, I believe it is a journey which ends in happiness. Death is a messenger of joy and like any messenger who brings good news I am eager to meet him."

"But if you go I will be very sad," protested Red Feather. "So I should go with you. I should meet the messenger and be happy, too. You have to take me with you!"

Dark Sky nodded in disagreement. "You and I are different. Once, long ago, I was as you are now: a child with taut skin and dark, shiny hair. I have traveled for many years and I have seen a great deal. Now I am old and there is nothing more of use to me here. That is why I am ready to die. But you are young and have much to do so you must stay."

"But sometimes little children go, too. I know they do. So why can't *I* go now? Oh, Great Grand-father, please, please don't go without me."

"You do not understand," nodded Dark Sky. "There is so much for you to do here—so much yet for you to learn."

Tears streamed down Red Feather's face. "But you have taught me everything, Great Grandfather. What am I going to learn without you? If you are going to die you have to take me with you. You have to!" Red Feather sobbed and he clutched the fingers of Dark Sky's weakened hand and squeezed them with all his strength.

Dark Sky sat up slightly. He slowly searched the darkening skies with his dull, tired eyes. Then he looked into the eyes of Red Feather. In a clear voice he said, "Listen and understand. This world can be very fearful. That is why you must draw close to the One Above and to the spiritual teachings He has given to men. As you journey through this world there will be times when your life is easy and filled with joy. At other times your life will be hard and very painful. If you do not give up during the difficult times, if you strive to overcome your trouble and sorrow, you will find strength within you that you did not know was there. Your own struggle will help you to understand the struggle of others and your heart will grow kind and pure. That heart, kind and pure and strong, will go with you when you go to meet the messenger of joy." Dark Sky sighed dryly. "But these are things which I cannot teach you. These things you must learn for yourself. Only when your heart has learned as much as it can in this world will you be called to the next. Not a season sooner will you go. Do you see now why you must stay in this world and I must go?"

A faint murmer crossed his lips. "I understand."

"Very good. But now," said Dark Sky and he gazed directly at him, ". . . you must say goodbye to me with great cheer and happiness for I am ready and the messenger of joy has been very patient with me."

Red Feather felt the strength leave his body. For a few moments he was silent, and then he answered. ". . . Goodbye, Great Grandfather."

"Goodbye," said Dark Sky and the many wrinkles around his mouth formed a gentle smile. "But are you crying, my courageous one?" Red Feather did not answer but Dark Sky did not scold. Instead, he reached out his hand. The young boy took it by the wrist and brought it up to his own face allowing it to catch the tear rolling past his upturned cheek.

"Come close," said Dark Sky. "Let me hug you once more—a hug that must last until we speak again."

Red Feather leaned forward. "But when, Great Grandfather; when will we speak again?"

"When your time comes," said Dark Sky, ". . . you and I will meet beyond the farthest horizon. But first there is much for you to do. Always remember that you are in this world for one reason: to purify your heart. There is no other purpose." Dark Sky's breathing suddenly became more ragged and his voice trembled. "First your heart must grow kind and pure . . ." he whispered. "Remember . . !"

Red Feather wrapped his arms around the shallow chest and thick blankets. He squeezed his eyes hard; the tears rolled freely.

Soon the breathing that sounded like dry wind stopped. Red Feather lay the bundle of blankets down flat on the cot and he watched as his hand grasped the blankets edge and covered a spiritless face of copper tones and long, white silk . . .

"Red Feather?" A voice called softly from behind him.

Red Feather rose to his feet and turned about. At the entrance of the tent stood Viola, a concerned look upon her face.

"All is well now," Red Feather said quietly. "Great Grandfather has gone to meet the messenger of joy." His cheeks were moist and though his eyes glistened with tears he smiled and looked directly into his sister's face.

As she stood in the space of the tent entrance, the light of the setting sun framed her slender figure and a soft, brown lustre reflected from her raven black hair.

SEVEN

Dark Sky was buried in the month of August on a piece of property situated a few miles beyond the reservation. His body was dressed in his ceremonial shirt and cuffs and carefully laid inside a simple stained wood coffin. Standing with his father and sister, their large adult hands gently holding each of his own, Red Feather watched the many faces of family and friends as they arrived and reverently formed a circle around the gravesite. David Austin and his mother were in the small crowd as were Aunt Louise and several other people from town. Nearly everyone on the reservation was present along with many relatives who had traveled great distances.

In the cool air of early morning they all gathered to pray and say farewell to a wise medicine man, a dear relative and a faithful friend who with eager anticipation had left for a great journey.

In a clear, resonant voice Red Feather's father chanted a traditional Arapaho prayer. Following the chant, several people stepped forward to speak of

Dark Sky, the way he had always helped them and how he had lived a long and unselfish life. "His radiance was like the sun," one of the older tribes people said. "I've known him all my life and I can tell you this: He had a very good spirit. His heart was kind and it was pure."

After the service people walked slowly back to their cars and pickups. No one looked sad or unhappy and many of them were smiling. Standing alone next to the simple grave marker, Red Feather easily recalled Dark Sky's words: "There is much for you to do. Always remember, you are in this world for one reason—to purify your heart . . ."

Red Feather took a deep breath. "I will remember."

EIGHT

The month of August ended all too soon and with September came the beginning of another school year. On the first morning, Red Feather carefully strapped on his new leather shoes, said goodbye to his father and Viola, and slowly walked across the fields towards town.

The skies were gray and smelled of rain. Stumbling down the incline to the river, Red Feather set down his notebook and from the damp bank picked up a small flat stone. For a moment he examined the smooth, curved edges with his wet fingers.

With a slicing motion of his arm, Red Feather tossed the stone so that it skipped over the surface of the water—three, four, five skips he counted— before it disappeared, exhausted, beneath the rippled surface.

Closing his eyes, Red Feather began to breathe deeply. Soon his mind was still.

It was September. The strange feeling of discomfort had vanished and with it a summer unlike any summer before had come to an end.

Of course some things had been the same as in past summers. Red Feather had played stickball, eaten ice cream and had gone to the movies more than once. In years to come, the stickball games and the ice cream of this particular summer would be forgotten. But something else had happened, too. Something that would be remembered.

Red Feather picked up his books and quickly began to climb the incline in the direction of the government school. He wondered what he would do today.

He wondered what lessons his heart would learn.

* * *